Infinite Collisions

poems by

Issa M. Lewis

Finishing Line Press
Georgetown, Kentucky

Infinite Collisions

Copyright © 2017 by Issa M. Lewis
ISBN 978-1-63534-181-2 First Edition
All rights reserved under International and Pan-American Copyright Conventions. No part of this book may be reproduced in any manner whatsoever without written permission from the publisher, except in the case of brief quotations embodied in critical articles and reviews.

Publisher: Leah Maines
Editor: Christen Kincaid
Cover Art: Ryan Lewis (Photographer)
Author Photo: Ryan Lewis (Photographer)
Cover Design: Elizabeth Maines

Printed in the USA on acid-free paper.
Order online: www.finishinglinepress.com
            also available on amazon.com

                    Author inquiries and mail orders:
                         Finishing Line Press
                           P. O. Box 1626
                      Georgetown, Kentucky 40324
                              U. S. A.

Table of Contents

The village of Grass Lake, population 1

On an uphill slope just east of town 2

In Michigan tradition, holes are dug 3

On this fertile ground, surrounded by sky 4

One day the townsmen built an iron road 5

In 1922 an heir is born 6

It's harvest time; pick up the pieces of 7

A.'s fingers do not tremble as she plies 8

Back home, life carries on as usual 9

What holds a house together? Is it wood 10

A spring wedding, and all around is white 11

Around the quilted bed, C.'s family stands 12

The picture starts to blur. Yellow and green 13

C.'s farm sheep in their pens, confused and tense 14

There are faces in the walls—not just pictures 15

The years are indifferent; they work on all 16

One day a dental practice came to town 17

At eighty-two years old, D. clambers up 18

The evening came when the warm lights stayed dark 19

There stands the old, half-rotted tractor shed 20

This book is dedicated to the Eschelbach family: Clarence and Amanda; their son Dean and his wife, Ella Mae; their grandchildren: Carol, Kay, Janice, and Gary; and their many great-grandchildren.

Special thanks to my husband, Ryan, for his unfaltering love and support; my sons Matthew and Ian for their endless, loving distractions; and my parents for instilling in me a belief that all things are possible. Finally, I would like to express my deep gratitude to Tayve Neese for her keen poetic insight and friendship.

I.

The village of Grass Lake, population:
barely. Long corn silk threads are ties that bind,
winding gravel paths a constellation
ribboning door to door. There is a kind

of peace in the night sky over small towns,
as barn doors close and farmers walk along
those paths to waiting windows, lights turned down
(some oil, some electric), a quiet song

on the radio. The sky is mirror
of what's below; faces turn up to see
the way from one star to another,
doorstep, doorknob, lock opened with a key.

Miles between each neighbor, a long night's walk:
they hold tight to corn kernels, grip the stalk.

II.

On an uphill slope just east of town,
The farmer C. surveys his new purchase:
green, rolling acres begging to be sown
with any seed to find a womb in this

dark, mothering topsoil. *Here is the place*
he thinks, *I'll build a barn, and there my home,*
a corncrib, a silo. He walks a pace,
the tall grass keeping record of his roam,

boot-steps initialing the ground, claiming
it now. A cricket song questions the sun
as it lowers itself, the sky flaming
into night. Hands in pockets, chewing gum,

C. turns on heel, heads for the gravel road,
towards his waiting truck, its ready load.

III.

In Michigan tradition, holes are dug
to hold the belly of the thing, the beams
reaching up to the sky like ribs to hug
the walls together, cinching up the seams.

The hole is dirt or mason block, its sides
mortared into their places by skilled hands.
Crawl down into the cool, damp underside
and fill it with blue glass and metal cans

as tokens of last year's lush, full harvest,
a spider furnace reaching soot-black arms
that shake and roar, the burn of coal expressed
in ire, in heat, a winter chill alarm.

This is the start of farmer C.'s new home:
man with a shovel, yielding earth, rich loam.

IV.

On this fertile ground, surrounded by sky
so blue a brown eye could get lost in it,
the farmer C. takes his young wife to lie
down in the fuzz-topped tall grass for a bit.

They gaze at clouds, name children yet to be
and draw them on her belly like a map
of fields: what seeds to use, what moon to see
at night for best planting. So soft, her lap,

he lays his head there, listening to the sounds
of growth, of promise burbling inside
of her like question marks: soft, sideways rounds
full up. They reach for each other and sigh.

Life all around them growing slow and green,
full of light, leaves press forward to be seen.

V.

One day the townsmen built an iron road
spiked right into the earth like a tattoo.
Daily the train arrived with heavy loads
to empty out beside and fill with new.

It snaked by north of town, chewing upon
abundant fields with its metallic tongue,
tasting the local flavors, pushing on
through green and gold and brown. Steam-filled song

ah-chuff, ah-chuff like the sighs of tired hills
allowing this intrusion; screaming brake
throws sparks that glow, then fade like passing thrills
It came to give. It also came to take.

This first contact: another world wants in.
It knocks, it rumbles, tastes like sweat and sin.

VI.

In 1922 an heir is born
into the quiet bedroom. Shafts of light
wrap their fingers around shades, dusty, worn,
as if to lay eyes on the humble sight:

a bare breast, sweaty hair pulled back in braids,
all motion ceased but for the tiny head
rooting, smelling his mother's skin. He's laid
upon her chest, warm, waiting to be fed.

The grandfather clock ticks by the minutes
of this new life. The baby finds his latch
and sighs with satisfaction, no limits
on his thirst. His mother, his truest match,

hums softly as she traces his soft shape,
temple to cheek, nose, chin, around to nape.

VII.

It's harvest time; pick up the pieces of
the year before they brown and sour in your
mouth. Pluck the berries, strip the corn with love
until your fingers crack. The work of hours

brings what will sustain them when the frost comes:
they'll can it, freeze it down below, sun-dry
it 'til the skin pulls edges into crumbs.
They'll stack it in the basement ceiling-high.

Outside the green is burning down to gold;
soon all will just be seed and chaff and ash.
Full-faced, the sun yields riches that they hold
with grateful, calloused hands, their winter cache.

Such tensile dirt, worked over like bread dough
until it rises, stretched, expanding, slow.

VIII.

A.'s fingers do not tremble as she plies
the needle, red thread weaving in and through;
anchoring with deft hands and restless eyes.
Sharp contrast, hard edge, but the line is true.

Yesterday, her son packed his duffel bag,
put on a brown jacket and pants, and stepped
off the front porch. His shoulders did not sag,
but pointed firmly east, composure kept.

She stitches a thick border together,
dangerous red against the field of white.
She slowly taps her toe and rocks her chair
to the rhythm of her sewing tonight.

But only when she sets the blue star's place
does she drop the needle, hide her face.

IX.

Back home, life carries on as usual,
as though there is no war, no reason to
change things. The fields, the plows, still usable;
the sheep still grow their fleece, the cows still moo.

E. patiently waits for the mail each day
for letters from North Africa (she thinks)—
the tiny scraps of soldier life that say
he's still alive; he breathes, he sneezes, blinks

himself awake each morning. The letter
arrives, stamped with official ink and holes
carved through his words so as not to let her
know position, orders, targets, or goals.

Between the words cut out, the man appears;
his yearning for a quiet night, a beer.

X.

What holds a house together? Is it wood
or plaster, brick or nails? How does one make
an angle, perfect square, as if one could
build such a thing—in nature, walls will take

the line they wish. So we impose ourselves
with tools and fixatives; we plumb our lines
with greatest care, use levels for our shelves
and cabinets. We make the world align

to us, make our houses in our image.
Then we pour ourselves into the blank space
between doorways: the start of our lineage
like sunlight through curtains of tea-dyed lace.

What holds a house together is the scent
of breakfast in a pan, bellies content.

XI.

A spring wedding, and all around is white:
the bride, the cherry tree in cloudy bloom,
the sheep—though dusty—hidden out of sight
behind barn doors. There stands the waiting groom,

fresh from the war, invisible scorch marks
on his face, on his hands; what he has seen
cannot be unraveled. Behind eyes, sparks
and haze. Men on the ground, a littered scene.

In front of him, a knowing face, soft hands.
It burns his throat like whiskey, this knowing
what will be now: not fire, but wedding bands
and quiet evenings, nowhere to be going

but to the comfort of a feather bed
that exhales welcome to a newlywed.

XII.

Around the quilted bed, C.'s family stands
like portraits of themselves, their faces worn
with waiting into maps of grief. Their hands
grasp anything they can: the quilt's torn

edge, their own mouths or temples, anything
to hold the moment and not drift away—
or is it C. who might slip? The late spring
light filters through the blinds and marks the day

as it rolls into dark. As the first sign
of starlight pricks the sky, the old man sighs
and shifts his head. His wife's hands, smooth and fine
despite their strength, brush the hair from his eyes.

the family is motionless, subdued;
strange how death makes the living breathless, too.

XIII.

The picture starts to blur. Yellow and green
human geometry that sprawled and climbed,
distinctive, edged—lines now cannot be seen
with clarity. The hawk's eye blinked, sun-blind

and there it went: those golden colors grayed
to asphalt, creeping over grass and earth,
intently rounding corners. Nothing stayed
its progress, like a slow, meandering birth.

Gravel roads were paved over, leveled flat
for tires where boots and hooves once crunched. The grass
browns at the edges, leans away from that
which would engulf it. Now the true impasse:

will the paver's brush spill paint and sprawl
or farmers sew new green, a living wall?

XIV.

C.'s farm sheep in their pens, confused and tense:
The cows across the field knew us. We let
them reach their heads between the fence
to nibble at our straw, their noses wet.

Sons helped their fathers, grandsons too, in spring
when the lambs came; gave milk to little ones
who lost their mothers. Rain and earth would bring
its own birth, succulent fields overgrown.

They kindly took our fleece in summer's throes,
got us through till fall, but where are the cows?
They've not been out since two spring-times ago.
The earth is hard and gray. Where are we now?

We see so little green, we wonder if we're
even still sheep without our fields to clear.

XV.

There are faces in the walls—not just pictures,
not the frames, but the walls themselves are full
of memories; one brother, three sisters:
D.'s children, and his wife's. Tiny hands pull

at pant legs, laughter echoes on the stair,
seeps into wallpaper. The time when K.
scratched the table, when son G. ate a pear
from the yard on a sticky summer day.

Are they ghosts? No, but whispers low and true
of what has been. A pen in hand records
each day, a child's first steps, and how he grew
and inks it on the walls, the floor, the doors.

Every brick and plank of wood in this place
holds tightly to each memory, each face.

XVI.

The years are indifferent; they work on all
of us without feeling. They bandage wounds
from lovers, friends, until the cuts are small
and neatly stitched, and therefore life resumes.

But those same years make slashes of their own
across our faces: near the mouth, the eyes,
webs of experience not easily sewn
together again. Time knows otherwise.

And on a town, also, the years can take
their toll. The buildings grow, the people come
to put down roots and make their home Grass Lake.
Fields spread, and roads entwine like lamb's wool spun.

The inevitable transformation
for better or for worse, no cessation.

XVII.

At eighty-two years old, D. clambers up
the faded red barn-side his father built
years before. From the roof, he sips a cup
of water from his thermos, minds the tilt—

a little steeper on northern side—
as he sits and takes in fields of corn and soy
just waking from their seed-beds, and a wide
enclosure where the sheep, gray-nosed, enjoy

what grass has dared to show. With one last look,
D. grabs his tools, begins to peel away
the shingles like pages of a yearbook.
He tosses them to the ground, where they lay

in piles, small slices of seasons long gone
remembering the rain, the snow, the sun.

XVIII.

One day, a dental practice came to town
and set up shop next door to D. He'd sold
the pieces of the farm, like seeds he'd sewn
and scattered all his life, raised to ripe old

age and harvested to sell at market.
The children gone, the last of the sheep, too;
empty barn with its trampled straw carpet.
One by one, each was gone, except for two:

the house and the old barn. Also, a half
of a u-shaped driveway that used to bend
back to the main road like an uneven bell graph,
now broken, a bent line, no distinct end.

The children all grew up and did not stay;
the city's concrete beckon ripped away.

XIX.

The evening came when the warm lights stayed dark
in D.'s front room, dark like the sky once was
before the city lights burned bright, a watermark
of human life, drowning out the stars.

The Adirondack chairs on the side porch
sit empty, purposeless as old tin cans.
Weeds in the yard as dry and stiff as starch
in the March thaw, crumpled like old plans

abandoned where the EMTs rushed in
and out again. Inside the house, it all
remains the same: expectant crossword, pen,
bifocals on the desk. A lone missed call

on the machine. The empty, dark windows
are left alone to live with their echoes.

XX.

There stands the old, half-rotted tractor shed
with wooden, graying slatted walls, the floor
gravel ground to dust. Hundreds of bumped heads
on the low beam walking through the door.

The wood croons creaking, low-toned whispers
of wet springs, snow-blind winters, early thaws;
lambs bleating for their milk, old transistors
humming. All reminders of what was:

a calendar from 1945,
sawhorses and their dust, a glass milk jar.
It's ghosts that keep a dying place alive
debris that brought them keeps them where they are.

Sit awhile in a corner and listen
to the dust motes' infinite collisions.

Issa M. Lewis is a graduate of the New England College MFA in Poetry program and was the 2013 recipient of the Lucille Clifton Poetry Prize awarded by Backbone Press. Her poems have appeared in *Pearl, Naugatuck River Review, Blue Lyra Review,* and many others. She currently teaches composition and professional writing at Davenport University and serves on the editorial board of Trio House Press, a small press publishing distinct voices in American poetry. She lives with her husband and two sons, enjoying every beautiful season in west Michigan.

www.ingramcontent.com/pod-product-compliance
Lightning Source LLC
LaVergne TN
LVHW041523070426
835507LV00012B/1788